DOG OR WOLF

BY BRENNA MALONEY

Children's Press®
An imprint of Scholastic Inc.

A special thank-you to the team at the Cincinnati Zoo & Botanical Garden for their expert consultation.

DOG

Library of Congress Cataloging-in-Publication Data available

ISBN 978-1-338-89980-1 (library binding) | ISBN 978-1-338-89981-8 (paperback)

10 9 8 7 6 5 4 3 2 1   24 25 26 27 28

Printed in China   62
First edition, 2024

Book design by Kay Petronio

Photos ©: cover left and throughout: Mike Linnane/500px/Getty Images; 4 right: Isselee/Dreamstime; 16–17: Peter Cade/Getty Images; 20–21 main: Roberto Machado Noa/Getty Images; 28 main: Stephen Simpson/Getty Images.
All other photos © Shutterstock.

WOLF

CONTENTS

MEET THE ANIMALS

Dogs and wolves are *very* different animals. Dogs are pets and live with people. Wolves are wild animals and live in nature. Wolves are taller than most dogs.

ADULT HUMAN

WOLF

DOG

The dog is a tame relative of the wolf. Wolves and dogs have a few things in common. They are both **canines**. And they are both **mammals**. Get ready to discover what dogs and wolves share and how they are different.

CHIHUAHUA

GRAY WOLF

FACT Chihuahuas are the smallest canine in the world. Wolves are the largest.

DOG CLOSE-UP

Dogs come in all shapes and sizes. They can be small and round or tall and thin. Their fur is called a coat. Coats can be smooth, short, silky, long, thick, or curly.

TAIL TALK

Dogs can show their feelings through their tails. A wagging tail might mean a dog is happy to see you.

COAT COLOR

Dog coats come in four main colors: black, brown, white, and red. These colors can have many shades. Some coats are a mixture of colors.

PAWS

Most dogs have five toes on their front paws and four toes on their back paws.

CHOMPERS

Adult dogs have about 42 teeth.

LISTEN UP!

Dogs hear sounds four times farther away than a human's ear can hear.

NOSE

Smell is a dog's strongest sense. The part of the brain connected to smell is 40 times larger in dogs than in humans.

TASTE BUDS

People have up to 10,000 taste buds. Dogs have only about 1,700. This might explain why dogs sometimes eat things we find gross!

GRAY WOLF

THICK FUR
Almost all wolves have thick fur that helps them live in cold places.

BUSHY TAILS
A wolf's tail is straight and does not curl like some dogs' tails.

LONG LEGS
The wolf is built for travel. Its legs are long, and it can walk at about 4 miles per hour (6 kph).

BIG FEET
Large paws with thick padding mean a wolf can travel in snow, like snowshoes!

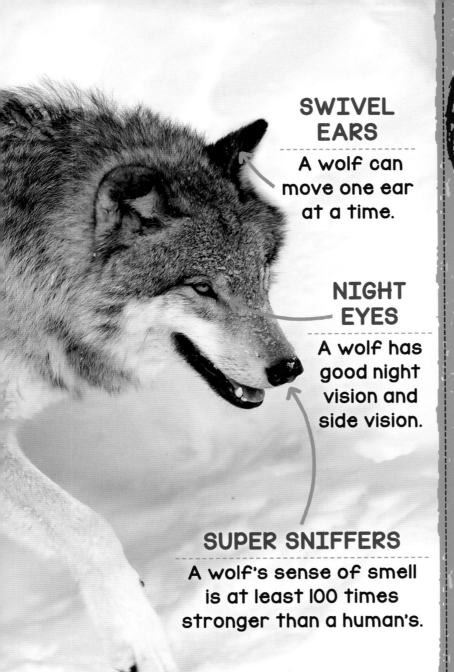

SWIVEL EARS

A wolf can move one ear at a time.

NIGHT EYES

A wolf has good night vision and side vision.

SUPER SNIFFERS

A wolf's sense of smell is at least 100 times stronger than a human's.

WOLF CLOSE-UP

Some wolves look like large dogs. The most common type of wolf is the gray wolf. It can weigh between 70 and 110 pounds (32 and 50 kg). The fur of a wolf is usually gray but may be brown, reddish, black, or even white.

Dogs are the most popular pet on the planet. **FACT**

BEST FRIENDS

There are hundreds of **breeds** of dogs. They can be found on every continent except Antarctica. Many dog breeds are able to survive on their own, whether it's in a forest or on city streets. Most dogs, however, are kept as pets. They fill many roles for people, such as hunting and protection.

IN THE WILD

Wolves can be found in the United States, Canada, and parts of Europe, Africa, and Asia. They live in many different types of natural **habitats**, especially forests. They also live in grasslands, deserts, and mountains. Wolves survive best in areas where there is enough **prey** to hunt and fewer people.

FACT Wolves can travel as many as 100 miles (161 km) in one day while hunting for food.

Dogs are **pack** animals by nature. A pack is a family group. Most dogs like hanging out with other dogs. A dog's human family becomes its pack.

The Labrador retriever is the most popular breed of pet dog in the world.

FACT

Wolves usually live in groups, or packs, of 6 to 10 animals. It is led by an **alpha** male and female. The pack includes their young and other adult wolves. The alpha male and female guide the pack. The pack works together as a team.

Onions, garlic, chocolate, grapes, and raisins can make a dog sick! **FACT**

DOGGIE DINNER

Dogs are **omnivores**. That means they eat meat and plants. In the wild, dogs mainly hunt small prey. They eat mice, rabbits, birds, and even insects. Pet dogs are usually fed wet or dry dog food. These foods are made from meat, chicken, fish, and some grains and vegetables. Some dogs also like fruit, such as bananas and blueberries.

DINING OUT

Wolves are **carnivores**. That means they eat meat. Wolves mostly hunt hooved mammals that are old, sick, or injured. They will eat deer, elk, moose, or bison. Wolves always hunt together to take down large animals they would not be able to overpower on their own.

The adult wolves in a pack will help feed any young pups.

COCKER SPANIEL

WOOF WOOF

Dogs use smells, sounds, and their bodies to speak. They bark, yip, and growl. They use body language by changing the position of their heads, necks, eyes, ears, and tails. Dogs don't just want to speak with other dogs. They want to speak with you, too!

CALL OF THE WILD

Wolves howl to speak to one another. A howl can locate pack members or be used to defend oneself. A wolf's howl can be heard up to 9 miles (14.5 km) away. Wolves speak in other ways, too. They growl, whimper, whine, and make a sound called a "huff-bark." They also use eye contact to talk to one another.

An angry wolf might
growl and show its teeth.

Puppies come in all sizes. Some pups weigh no more than a carton of milk. **FACT**

PUPPY POWER

A mother dog can have a **litter** of puppies twice a year. Puppies are born with a strong sense of smell, but they can't open their eyes right away. Puppies grow quickly. Most will double their birth weight after the first *week*! Between two and four weeks old, they usually begin to growl, bite, wag their tails, and bark.

WOLF PUPS

Wolf babies are born in early spring in litters of four to six pups. They are usually born in a **den**. At birth, pups cannot see or hear. They stay in the den for about six weeks but are cared for by the entire pack. By around eight months old, the pups begin traveling with the adults and learning how to hunt. Wolves stay with the pack until they are about three years old.

When it is born, a wolf pup weighs about as much as a loaf of bread.

NIGHTY NIGHT

Dogs usually sleep between 12 and 14 hours in a day. Most sleep at night when their family sleeps. But they also take little naps during the day.

FACT

Scientists think that both wolves and dogs dream when they sleep.

Wolves are most active before sunrise and sunset. They sleep during the day. Gray wolves sleep between six and eight hours per day.

YOU DECIDE!

Now you know what makes dogs and wolves so different! If you had to choose, would you rather be a dog or a wolf? If you want your dinner served to you in a bowl by people, you may choose to be a dog. If you wanted to be a meat eater that travels in a pack, you might want to be a wolf.

GLOSSARY

alpha (AL-fuh) – the top-ranking wolf in a pack

breed – a particular type of plant or animal

canine (KAY-nine) – an animal belonging to a family of mammals that includes dogs and wolves

carnivore (KAHR-nuh-vor) – an animal that eats meat

den – the home of a wild animal, such as a wolf

habitat (HAB-i-tat) – the place where an animal or plant is usually found

litter (LIT-ur) – a number of baby animals that are born at the same time to the same mother

mammal (MAM-uhl) – a warm-blooded animal that has hair or fur and usually gives birth to live babie

omnivore (AHM-nuh-vor) – an animal that eats both plants and meat

pack (pak) – a group of similar animals

prey (pray) – an animal that is hunted by another animal for food

INDEX

ABOUT THE AUTHOR

Brenna Maloney is the author of many books. She lives and works in Washington, DC, with her husband, two sons, one dog, two pet cats, but no wolves. If she had to choose, she would want to be a pug.